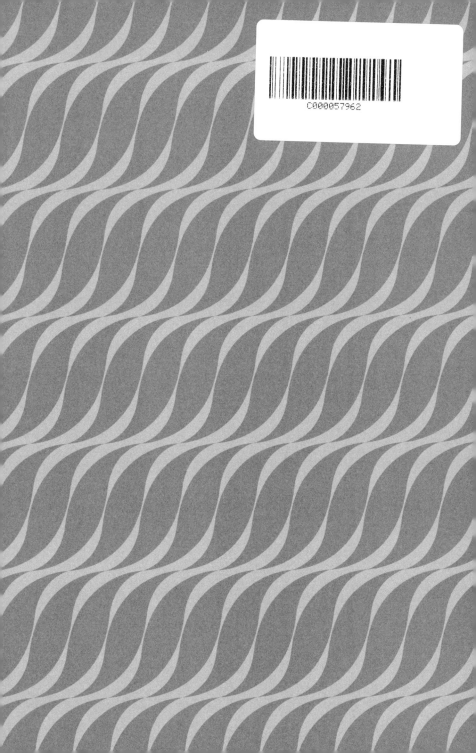

BEST OF IRELAND

Matthew Drennan

southwater

Contents

Introduction

The Irish are a hospitable people, and sharing a meal with family and friends is an integral part of their lives in cities and villages alike. Food is unfussy, and dishes are often hearty and substantial. They all have one thing in common – the freshest and best of seasonal ingredients. The fertile soil ensures a ready supply of excellent beef, dairy products and vegetables. An island with miles of coastline and an extensive network of unpolluted rivers and lakes, Ireland is bountifully supplied with superb fish and seafood.

Potatoes are to the Irish what pasta is to the Italians and rice to the Chinese. In the past, the potato was almost all the poor had to eat; bleak necessity has given rise to a vast repertoire of tasty recipes using this versatile vegetable, including savoury soups, delicious side dishes and mouthwatering desserts.

This book includes all the classic dishes and traditional favourites, as well as many other recipes for all courses and occasions, from heartwarming soups to delicate desserts and delicious breads. A collection of side dishes using the potato is also included. Irish food is good food in the truest sense of the word and the best of it is very good indeed.

Ingredients

Meat & Poultry

Irish beef is world-famous for its superb quality. Both baby and yearling lambs are produced and most chickens and turkeys are free-range. Pork features less in Irish cooking, except in the form of bacon and gammon.

Fish & Seafood

Ireland is well-known for its excellent salmon. Other popular fish include plaice, cod and brill. Smoked fish is a speciality of some coastal areas, especially in County Cork. The choice of seafood is extensive – fresh mussels, clams, lobster, crab and prawns, including Dublin Bay prawns, are widely available. Oysters feature in the traditional Guinness & Oyster Pie, but this is no longer the inexpensive meal it once was.

Crab

Dublin Bay Prawns

Vegetables & Fruit

Potatoes are paramount, and floury varieties are the most popular. Waxy varieties are called "soapy" by the Irish. Cabbage probably ranks second in importance, closely followed by root

Cabbage

Carrots

vegetables, such as carrots, turnips and swedes. Other widely grown vegetables include onions, leeks, peas and beans.

Leek

Seasonal fruits are popular as summer desserts and include gooseberries, strawberries, blackberries, plums and raspberries. Apples and pears are also cultivated.

Apples

Dairy Products

Irish butter and cream have a well-deserved reputation and, even in these days of cholesterol awareness and low-fat cooking, are often included in a wide variety of dishes. Irish cheeses include Cashel Blue from Tipperary, Milleens from County Cork and St Killian from County Wexford.

Herbs & Flavourings

In many parts of Ireland, herbs, including garlic, grow wild. Parsley, chives, thyme and mint are the most popular flavourings.

Carragheen moss is a reddish purple seaweed harvested on the west coast of Ireland. It is rich in a natural gelling agent and minerals. It can be eaten as a

vegetable like spinach, but is also available dried to a yellowish pink colour and used as a thickening agent. It is available from health food shops.

Young wild nettles are also harvested, especially in the spring. Only the tender young tips are used as the lower leaves and stems are too tough. If picking wild nettles, wear protective gloves and choose plants well away from traffic pollution.

Sorrel is another wild herb which is used in Irish cooking. It has a refreshing lemony flavour and can be used in salads, soups and sauces.

Above: The popular and versatile potato is used in many traditional Irish recipes.

Drinks

Ireland has a venerable history of brewing and stout accounts for about half of all the beer sold in the country. Besides enjoying a convivial pint or two in the pub, the Irish also cook with it, classically combining it with beef and with oysters. The Guinness Brewery in Dublin is now world-famous. Other popular Irish stouts are produced by Beamish and Crawford and by Murphy's, both in Cork.

Techniques

Cleaning Potatoes

Locally grown potatoes from a farm shop or home-grown potatoes may still have some earth attached to them.

1 If the potatoes are dirty, use a small scrubbing brush or a gentle scourer to clean them. This will also remove the peel of new potatoes.

2 Remove any green or discoloured patches or black eyes carefully, using a sharp pointed knife or potato peeler, unless you are going to peel them after cooking.

Peeling Potatoes

Much of the goodness and flavour of a potato is in the skin and just below it.

1 Use a very sharp potato peeler to remove the thinnest layer possible in long even strips.

2 If you cook unpeeled potatoes and want to peel them immediately, hold the hot potato with a fork and gently peel off the skin.

Slicing Potatoes

Try to cut all the slices the same thickness so that they cook evenly.

1 Put the tip of the knife on the work surface or board first, then press the heel of the knife down firmly to create even slices.

Dicing Potatoes

If the recipe calls for dice, this means you have to be more precise and cut the potato into evenly shaped cubes.

1 Trim the potato into a neat rectangle first (keep the outside pieces for mash, or to add to a soup), then cut the rectangles into thick, even slices.

2 Turn the stack of slices over and cut into thick batons and finally into even cubes of the size needed for the recipe you are using.

Boiling Potatoes

1 Place the potatoes in a large pan and just cover with lightly salted water and a tight-fitting lid. Bring to the boil over a gentle heat and boil gently for 15–20 minutes. Boiling too fast tends to cook the potato on the outside first so it becomes mushy and falls apart before the middle is cooked.

2 Drain the potatoes through a colander and then return them to the pan to dry off.

Chopping Onions

Many dishes use chopped onions as an essential flavouring. Onions can be finely chopped easily and quickly using this method.

1 Peel the onion. Cut it in half and set it cut side down on a board. Make lengthways vertical cuts along it, cutting almost but not quite through to the root.

2 Make two horizontal cuts from the stalk end towards the root, but not through it. Cut the onion crossways to form small, even dice.

Steaming Potatoes This gentle way of cooking is particularly good for very floury potatoes and those which fall apart easily.

Chopping Herbs

Chop herbs just before you use them: the flavour will then be at its best.

1 Place the leaves on a clean, dry board. Use a large, sharp cook's knife (if you use a blunt knife you will bruise the herbs rather than slice them) and chop them until they are as coarse or as fine as needed.

2 Alternatively, use a herb chopper, also called a *mezzaluna,* which is a very useful tool for finely chopping herbs or vegetables and consists of a sharp, curved blade with two handles. Use the *mezzaluna* in a seesaw motion for best results.

Leek & Thyme Soup

A filling, heart-warming soup which can be processed to a smooth purée or served as it is here, in its original peasant style.

Serves 4

INGREDIENTS
900 g/2 lb leeks
450 g/1 lb potatoes
115 g/4 oz/½ cup butter
1 large fresh thyme sprig
300 ml/½ pint/1¼ cups
    semi-skimmed milk
salt and freshly ground
    black pepper
thyme leaves, to garnish (optional)
60 ml/4 tbsp double cream,
    to serve

3 Cover and cook for 4–5 minutes, until softened. Add the potato pieces and just enough cold water to cover the vegetables. Cover and cook over a low heat for 30 minutes.

4 Pour in the semi-skimmed milk and the seasoning, cover and simmer for a further 30 minutes. You will find that some of the potato breaks up leaving you with a semi-purée and rather lumpy soup.

1 Top and tail the leeks. If you are using big winter leeks strip away the coarser outer leaves before cutting the leeks into thick slices. Wash under cold running water.

2 Peel the potatoes and cut them into rough dice, about 2.5 cm/1 in, and dry thoroughly on kitchen paper. Melt the butter in a large saucepan and add the leeks and the thyme sprig.

5 Remove the thyme sprig, and serve, adding a spoon of double cream and a garnish of thyme leaves to each portion, if using.

Pea & Ham Soup

This substantial soup is based on the classic partnership of peas and ham and is packed with flavour. Delicious served with crusty bread.

Serves 4

INGREDIENTS
450 g/1 lb/2½ cups green
    split peas
4 rindless streaky bacon rashers
1 onion, roughly chopped
2 carrots, sliced
1 celery stick, sliced
2.4 litres/4¼ pints/10½ cups
    cold water
1 fresh thyme sprig
2 bay leaves
1 large potato, roughly diced
1 bacon hock
freshly ground black pepper

1 Put the split peas into a bowl, cover with cold water and leave to soak overnight. Drain.

2 Cut the streaky bacon rashers into small pieces. In a large saucepan, dry fry the bacon for 4–5 minutes, or until crisp. Remove from the pan with a slotted spoon.

VARIATION: The main ingredient for this dish is bacon hock, which is the narrow piece of bone cut from a leg of ham. You could use a piece of belly of pork instead, if you like, and remove it before serving the finished soup.

3 Add the chopped onion, sliced carrots and celery to the pan and cook for 3–4 minutes, until the onion is softened, but not brown. Return the bacon to the pan with the water.

4 Add the split peas, thyme, bay leaves, potato and bacon hock to the pan. Bring to the boil, reduce the heat, cover and cook gently for 1 hour.

5 Remove the thyme, bay leaves and hock. Process the soup in a blender or food processor until smooth. Return to a clean pan. Cut the meat from the hock and add to the soup. Season with plenty of black pepper and serve.

Yellow Broth

This famous Northern Irish soup is thickened with oatmeal which also adds to its flavour. It makes a hearty and nutritious lunch.

Serves 4

INGREDIENTS
25 g/1 oz/2 tbsp butter
1 onion, finely chopped
1 celery stick, finely chopped
1 carrot, finely chopped
25 g/1 oz/¼ cup plain flour
900 ml/1½ pints/3¾ cups
   chicken stock
25 g/1 oz/¼ cup medium oatmeal
115 g/4 oz spinach, chopped
30 ml/2 tbsp cream
salt and freshly ground
   black pepper

1 Melt the butter in a large saucepan. Add the onion, celery and carrot, and cook for about 2 minutes, until the onion is soft.

2 Stir in the flour and cook gently for a further minute, stirring constantly. Pour in the chicken stock, bring to the boil and cover. Reduce the heat and simmer for 30 minutes, until the vegetables are tender.

3 Stir in the oatmeal and chopped spinach and cook for a further 15 minutes, stirring occasionally.

4 Stir in the cream and season well. Serve with a grinding of black pepper.

Nettle Soup

A country-style soup which is a tasty variation of the classic Irish potato soup incorporating tender nettle tops. Serve with crusty bread.

Serves 4

INGREDIENTS
115 g/4 oz/½ cup butter
450 g/1 lb large onions, sliced
450 g/1 lb potatoes, cut into chunks
750 ml/1¼ pints/3 cups chicken stock
25 g/1 oz young nettle leaves
small bunch of fresh chives, snipped
salt and freshly ground black pepper
double cream, to serve

1 Melt the butter in a large saucepan and add the sliced onions. Cover and cook for 5 minutes, until just softened. Add the potatoes to the saucepan with the chicken stock. Cover and cook for 25 minutes.

2 Wearing rubber gloves, remove the nettle leaves from their stalks. Wash the leaves under cold running water, then dry on kitchen paper. Add to the saucepan and cook for a further 5 minutes.

3 Ladle the soup into a blender or food processor and process until smooth. Return to a clean saucepan and season well. Stir in the chives and serve with a swirl of cream and a sprinkling of pepper.

COOK'S TIP: Collect nettle tops in spring when the plants are up to 20 cm/8 in high. Wear gloves for this.

Celery Soup

Mild celery with a hint of nutmeg – this classic creamy soup makes a perfect starter served with wholemeal bread.

Serves 4

INGREDIENTS
1 small head of celery
1 onion, finely chopped
1 small garlic clove, crushed
few fresh parsley sprigs
2 bay leaves
1 fresh thyme sprig
600 ml/1 pint/2½ cups
   semi-skimmed milk
25 g/1 oz/2 tbsp butter, softened
25 g/1 oz/¼ cup plain flour
pinch of grated nutmeg
1 egg yolk, beaten
salt and freshly ground
   black pepper
chopped fresh parsley,
   to garnish
croûtons, to serve

1 Break the head of celery into sticks and wash thoroughly. Trim the root ends. Chop the sticks and leaves and put them into a large saucepan.

VARIATION: If you do not have a blender or food processor, pass the soup through a metal sieve, pressing the cooked vegetables through with the back of a spoon.

2 Add the chopped onion, garlic, parsley, bay leaves, thyme and just enough water to cover. Bring to the boil and simmer the vegetables, uncovered, over a gentle heat for about 35 minutes.

3 In a clean saucepan, bring the semi-skimmed milk to the boil. Knead the butter and flour together to make a roux and whisk into the hot milk until just thickened. Cook over a gentle heat for about 10 minutes, stirring occasionally. Pour into the celery mixture and cook for 5 minutes.

4 Remove the bay leaves and thyme. Using a ladle, spoon the soup into a blender or food processor and process for 1 minute, until smooth. Return to a clean saucepan and season well. Stir in the nutmeg and beaten egg yolk. Bring almost to boiling point, then serve garnished with parsley and croûtons.

Plaice in a Green Jacket

Fresh fillets of plaice, wrapped in lettuce, gently poached and served with a buttery white wine sauce.

Serves 4

INGREDIENTS
4 fresh plaice fillets, about 175 g/6 oz each
1 large head of round lettuce
2 shallots, finely chopped
1 bay leaf
300 ml/½ pint/1¼ cups dry white wine
275 g/10 oz/1¼ cups unsalted butter,
    softened, plus extra, for greasing
15 ml/1 tbsp snipped fresh chives
salt and freshly ground black pepper
boiled potatoes, to serve (optional)

1 Preheat the oven to 180°C/350°F/ Gas 4. Using a very sharp knife, skin the plaice fillets. Insert the blade of the knife between the skin and the fillet at the tail end, then, holding the skin with one hand, glide the knife along the skin to remove the fillet.

> VARIATION: This recipe would also work well with lemon sole fillets instead of the plaice.

2 Bring a large saucepan of water to the boil. Separate the lettuce leaves and drop them into the water for 1 minute. Remove with a slotted spoon and refresh under cold water. Drain well.

3 Lay out 3–4 leaves and put a plaice fillet on top. Season well and wrap the leaves around each fish. Top with more leaves, if necessary. Put the fish into a large buttered dish and pour in a little water. Cover with buttered paper and cook in the oven for 15 minutes.

4 Meanwhile, put the shallots, bay leaf and white wine into a saucepan. Cook over a high heat for 5 minutes, until reduced to about 60–75 ml/4–5 tbsp.

5 Remove the bay leaf. Whisk in the butter, a little at a time, until the sauce is smooth and glossy. Strain into a clean pan. Stir in the chives and season well. Do not boil. Lift the wrapped fish out of the dish and serve with the sauce and boiled potatoes, if liked.

Salmon with Sorrel

A luxurious, yet light, combination of flavours makes this dish delectable.

Serves 4

INGREDIENTS
225 g/8 oz fish bones
1 small onion, sliced
3–4 peppercorns
1 bay leaf
few fresh parsley stalks
300 ml/½ pint/1¼ cups cold water
25 g/1 oz/2 tbsp butter, melted
4 salmon fillets, about 175 g/6 oz each
120 ml/4 fl oz/½ cup dry white wine
300 ml/½ pint/1¼ cups single cream
75 g/3 oz fresh sorrel, washed
salt and freshly ground black pepper

1 Preheat the oven to 200°C/400°F/
Gas 6. Wash the fish bones and put
into a saucepan with the onion,
peppercorns, bay leaf and parsley stalks.

2 Add the cold water. Bring to the
boil, reduce the heat and simmer for
20 minutes.

3 Brush an ovenproof dish with some
of the butter. Add the salmon and
brush with the remaining butter. Bake
for 10 minutes, until just cooked.

4 Meanwhile, strain 150 ml/¼ pint/
⅔ cup of the stock into a saucepan.
Add the wine and cook over a high
heat until the liquid is reduced by half.

5 Pour in the cream and bring to the
boil. Reduce the heat and simmer
until the sauce just coats a spoon, then
season. Tear the sorrel into pieces and
add to the sauce. Cook for 1 minute.
Serve with the salmon.

Cod with Parsley Sauce

A traditional accompaniment for this tasty dish would be cooked cabbage.

Serves 4

INGREDIENTS

25 g/1 oz/2 tbsp butter, plus extra for greasing
4 cod fillets or steaks, about 225 g/8 oz each
1 bay leaf
6 peppercorns
small bunch of fresh parsley, stalks removed,
  leaves chopped
1 shallot, quartered
25 g/1 oz/¼ cup plain flour
300 ml/½ pint/1¼ cups semi-skimmed milk
salt and freshly ground black pepper

1 Grease a large flameproof casserole with a little butter. Lay the four cod fillets in the base, skin side down. Add the bay leaf, peppercorns, parsley stalks and the shallot.

2 Cover the fish with cold water. Bring to the boil over a low heat, then simmer very gently for 5 minutes.

3 Melt the butter in a saucepan, stir in the flour and cook gently for 1 minute. Strain the stock from the fish and reserve 150 ml/¼ pint/⅔ cup. Remove the fish from the casserole and keep warm. Gradually add the reserved stock to the flour mixture and continue stirring over a medium heat until smooth and thickened.

4 Gradually add the milk and bring to the boil. Reduce the heat and cook for 10 minutes, stirring occasionally. Add the chopped parsley, season and serve with the fish.

Wrapped Salmon & Rice

This dish is made with chunks of fresh salmon, combined with mushrooms, eggs and rice in light and flaky pastry.

Serves 4

INGREDIENTS
450 g/1 lb skinned and boned fresh
  salmon fillet
115 g/4 oz/1½ cups button mushrooms
6 spring onions
50 g/2 oz/4 tbsp butter
2 eggs, hard-boiled
175 g/6 oz/1 cup long grain rice, cooked
juice of ½ lemon
450 g/1 lb puff pastry, thawed
  if frozen
1 egg, beaten
salt and freshly ground black pepper
hollandaise sauce, to serve

1 Preheat the oven to 200°C/400°F/ Gas 6. Put the salmon into a saucepan with just enough water to cover it. Poach it gently for 10 minutes, until just cooked. Drain and leave to cool.

COOK'S TIP: To make hollandaise sauce, put 30 ml/2 tbsp each white wine vinegar and water, 1 bay leaf and 6 peppercorns in a saucepan and boil until reduced by half. Strain into a heatproof bowl set over a pan of gently simmering water and stir in 4 egg yolks. Remove from the heat and cook, stirring constantly, for 8–10 minutes, until glossy and slightly thickened. Season to taste.

2 Roughly chop the mushrooms and finely slice the spring onions. Melt the butter in a saucepan and cook the mushrooms and spring onions for 2–3 minutes. Place them in a bowl.

3 Flake the fish and add to the mushroom and onion mixture. Chop the eggs and stir into the salmon mixture with the rice. Stir in the lemon juice and season well.

4 Roll out the pastry to a rectangle 30 x 35 cm/12 x 14 in. Brush the edges with egg. Spoon the filling into the centre of the pastry. Join the edges and seal the sides and ends with egg.

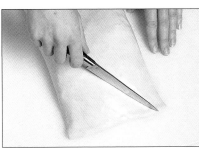

5 Score the top of the pastry with a knife and brush with the remaining egg. Bake for about 30 minutes, until golden. Serve hot with hollandaise sauce, or leave to cool completely and serve cold.

Seafood Pie

There are as many variations of this dish as there are fish in the sea – use whatever is fresh and available.

Serves 4

INGREDIENTS
450 g/1 lb fish bones, cleaned
6 peppercorns
1 small onion, sliced
1 bay leaf
750 ml/1¼ pints/3 cups cold water
900 g/2 lb smoked haddock
225 g/8 oz raw prawns
450 g/1 lb live mussels, cleaned
675 g/1½ lb potatoes
65 g/2½ oz/5 tbsp butter plus extra,
    for greasing
25 g/1 oz/¼ cup plain flour
350 g/12 oz leeks, sliced
115 g/4 oz/1½ cups sliced button mushrooms
15 ml/1 tbsp chopped fresh tarragon
15 ml/1 tbsp chopped fresh parsley
salt and freshly ground black pepper
fresh tarragon, to garnish

1 Put the fish bones, peppercorns, onion and bay leaf into a small saucepan with the cold water. Bring to the boil, reduce the heat and simmer for 20 minutes. Remove from the heat and set aside.

2 Put the smoked haddock into a pan with water to cover it. Cover with a piece of buttered greaseproof paper and simmer for 15 minutes. Drain and cool, then remove the bones and skin and put the flaked fish into a bowl.

3 Drop the prawns into a pan of boiling water and cook until they begin to float. Drain and refresh under cold running water. Peel and add the prawns to the bowl of flaked fish.

4 Place the mussels in a saucepan with 30 ml/2 tbsp water. Cover and cook over a high heat for 5–6 minutes, until the mussels have opened. Discard any that have not. Refresh under cold water and remove the shells. Put the cooked mussels into the bowl with the fish.

5 Boil the potatoes for 20 minutes. Drain and dry over a high heat for 1 minute. Season and mash with 25 g/1 oz/2 tbsp of the butter.

6 Meanwhile, melt 25 g/1 oz/2 tbsp of the butter in a saucepan. Stir in the flour and cook for 1 minute. Strain the fish stock and measure 600 ml/1 pint/2½ cups. Whisk a little at a time into the roux until smooth. Cook over a low heat for 10 minutes.

7 Preheat the oven to 180°C/350°F/ Gas 4. Melt the remaining butter in another saucepan, add the leeks and mushrooms and cook for 4–5 minutes, taking care not to brown them. Add to the fish. Stir in the chopped herbs.

8 Pour in the sauce and fold together. Adjust the seasoning, then spoon into a pie dish. Spoon over the mashed potatoes and smooth level with a fork. Place in the oven and cook for 30 minutes. Garnish with the tarragon.

Prawns with Garlic Breadcrumbs

Fresh Dublin Bay prawns are a delight when smothered in garlic butter.

Serves 4

INGREDIENTS
32 Dublin Bay prawns
350 g/12 oz/1½ cups butter, softened
8 garlic cloves, chopped
30 ml/2 tbsp chopped fresh parsley
4 spring onions, finely chopped
15 ml/1 tbsp wholegrain mustard
115 g/4 oz/2 cups fresh white breadcrumbs
freshly ground black pepper
fresh parsley, to garnish
brown bread, to serve

1 Bring a large pan of water to the boil. Drop in the prawns. Cook until they float on top of the water. Drain and refresh under cold water.

2 Peel all but four of the prawns. Preheat the oven to 200°C/400°F/ Gas 6. Place the butter, garlic, parsley, spring onions, mustard and plenty of pepper in a bowl. Beat until well blended.

3 Divide the peeled prawns among four individual ovenproof dishes. Divide the butter among them and spread it over the prawns. Sprinkle with the fresh breadcrumbs.

4 Bake for about 15 minutes, or until the breadcrumbs are golden brown. Garnish with fresh parsley and the unpeeled prawns, and serve with brown bread.

Hot Dressed Crab

This dish has topped the menu in Irish restaurants for many years.

Serves 4

INGREDIENTS
150 ml/¼ pint/⅔ cup milk
40 g/1½ oz/3 tbsp butter
15 ml/1 tbsp plain flour
350 g/12 oz fresh white crab meat
5 ml/1 tsp French mustard
275 g/10 oz/5 cups fresh breadcrumbs
30 ml/2 tbsp snipped
   fresh chives
salt and freshly ground
   black pepper
snipped fresh chives and chopped fresh
   parsley, to garnish

1 Preheat the oven to 200°C/400°F/ Gas 6. Bring the milk to the boil.

2 In another saucepan, melt 15 g/ ½ oz/1 tbsp of the butter. Stir in the flour and cook for 1 minute. Gradually whisk in the milk, a little at a time, until smooth and thick. Cook over a gentle heat for 5 minutes. Allow to cool.

3 Put the crab meat into a bowl with the mustard, 150 g/5 oz/2½ cups of the breadcrumbs and the snipped chives. Season and stir into the sauce.

4 Spoon the mixture into four crab shells or ovenproof dishes. Sprinkle with the remaining breadcrumbs and dot with the remaining butter. Bake for 20 minutes. Serve garnished with the chives and parsley.

Roast Chicken with Herb & Orange Bread Stuffing

This orange-scented chicken can be served with potatoes and roasted onions.

Serves 4–6

INGREDIENTS
2 onions
about 25 g/1 oz/2 tbsp butter
150 g/5 oz/2½ cups soft white breadcrumbs
30 ml/2 tbsp chopped fresh mixed herbs
grated rind of 1 orange
1.5 kg/3–3½ lb chicken with giblets
1 carrot, sliced
1 bay leaf
1 fresh thyme sprig
900 ml/1½ pints/3¾ cups cold water
15 ml/1 tbsp tomato purée
10 ml/2 tsp cornflour, mixed with
    15 ml/1 tbsp cold water
salt and freshly ground black pepper
chopped fresh thyme, to garnish

1 Preheat the oven to 200°C/400°F/ Gas 6. Finely chop one onion. Melt the butter in a pan and add the onion. Cook for 3–4 minutes, until soft. Stir in the breadcrumbs, fresh herbs and orange rind. Season well.

2 Remove the giblets from the chicken and put aside. Wash the cavity of the chicken and dry well with kitchen paper. Spoon in the herb and orange stuffing, then rub a little butter into the breast and season it well. Put the chicken into a roasting tin and cook in the oven for 20 minutes, then reduce the heat to 180°C/350°F/ Gas 4 and cook for a further hour.

3 Put the giblets, the other onion, the carrot, bay leaf, thyme and cold water into a large pan. Bring to the boil then skim off the scum. Simmer while the chicken is roasting.

4 Remove the chicken from the tin. Skim off the fat from the cooking juices, strain the juices and stock into a pan and discard the giblets and vegetables. Simmer for about 5 minutes more. Whisk in the tomato purée.

5 Whisk the cornflour paste into the gravy and cook for 1 minute. Season well. Serve the roast chicken, garnished with thyme and accompanied by the gravy, served separately.

Chicken, Leek & Bacon Casserole

A moist whole chicken, braised on a bed of leeks and bacon and topped with a creamy tarragon sauce.

Serves 4–6

INGREDIENTS
15 ml/1 tbsp vegetable oil
25 g/1 oz/2 tbsp butter
1.5 kg/3–3½ lb chicken
225 g/8 oz streaky bacon
450 g/1 lb leeks
250 ml/8 fl oz/1 cup chicken stock
250 ml/8 fl oz/1 cup double cream
15 ml/1 tbsp chopped fresh tarragon
salt and freshly ground
    black pepper

1 Preheat the oven to 180°C/350°F/Gas 4. Heat the oil and butter in a large, flameproof casserole. Add the chicken and cook it, breast side down, for 5 minutes, until golden. Remove from the casserole.

2 Roughly dice the bacon and add to the casserole. Cook for 4–5 minutes, until golden.

3 Top and tail the leeks, cut them into 2.5 cm/1 in pieces and add to the bacon. Cook for 5 minutes until the leeks begin to brown. Put the chicken on top of the bacon and leeks. Cover and cook in the oven for 1½ hours.

4 Remove the chicken, bacon and leeks from the casserole. Skim the fat from the juices. Pour in the stock and the cream and bring to the boil. Cook for 4–5 minutes, until slightly reduced and thickened.

5 Stir in the tarragon and seasoning (it may only need pepper). Slice the chicken and serve with the bacon, leeks and a little sauce.

COOK'S TIP: Young leeks have a delicate flavour. If using older leeks, remove any woody core, and use mostly the white part.

Coddle

There are numerous variations of this traditional favourite dish, but the basic ingredients are always potatoes, sausages and bacon.

Serves 4

INGREDIENTS
4 back bacon rashers
15 ml/1 tbsp vegetable oil
2 large onions, chopped
2 garlic cloves, crushed
8 large pork sausages
4 large potatoes
1.5 ml/¼ tsp dried sage
300 ml/½ pint/1¼ cups chicken stock
freshly ground black pepper
30 ml/2 tbsp chopped
   fresh parsley, to garnish
soda bread, to serve

1 Preheat the oven to 180°C/350°F/ Gas 4. Cut the bacon rashers into 2.5 cm/1 in strips.

2 Heat the oil in a frying pan and fry the bacon for 2 minutes. Add the onions and cook for a further 5–6 minutes, until golden. Add the garlic and cook for 1 minute, then remove from the pan and set aside.

3 Add the pork sausages to the frying pan and cook on all sides for about 5–6 minutes, until golden brown.

4 Slice the potatoes thinly and arrange in the base of a large, buttered ovenproof dish. Spoon the bacon and onion mixture on top. Season with pepper and sprinkle with the sage.

5 Put the sausages on the top, and pour over the chicken stock. Cover and cook in the oven for 1 hour. Sprinkle with parsley, and serve with fresh soda bread.

COOK'S TIP: Virtually every Irish butcher has his own recipe for sausages. If you can find these kinds of sausages, you will certainly notice the difference. Alternatively, try some of the newer, more interesting sausages available in supermarkets. They won't be authentic, but will often taste delicious.

Boiled Ham & Cabbage

A no-nonsense dish that is full of warming winter flavours and very easy to make. This makes a substantial midweek supper.

Serves 6

INGREDIENTS

1.25 kg/2¾ lb ham, in one piece, soaked
    overnight (see Cook's Tip)
2 bay leaves
12 peppercorns
1 celery stick, halved
1–2 onions, halved
2 large carrots
1 large Savoy cabbage
salt and freshly ground black pepper
chopped fresh parsley, to garnish
boiled potatoes, to serve (optional)

1 Drain the water from the ham if you have soaked it. Tie the meat then weigh it to calculate the cooking time. Put the ham into a large saucepan and cover with cold water.

2 Add the bay leaves, peppercorns, celery stick, onions and carrots. Bring to the boil, reduce the heat, cover and simmer for 25 minutes per 450 g/1 lb plus 25 minutes.

3 Carefully lift out the ham and set it aside. Drain the cooking liquid into a clean saucepan and bring to the boil.

4 Meanwhile, discard the outer leaves of the cabbage. Tear the remaining leaves, including the heart, into pieces, discarding any of the tough stalks. Add to the cooking liquid and cook, uncovered, for 20 minutes, until tender. Taste for seasoning – you may not have to add any.

5 Serve slices of the warm ham on a bed of cabbage with a little of the cooking liquid poured over the top. Garnish with the chopped parsley and serve with boiled potatoes, if liked.

COOK'S TIP: It is always difficult to tell how salty a piece of ham is going to be unless you buy it from a regular source. If in doubt, soak it in cold water for several hours or overnight, changing the water at least once.

Irish Stew

Simple and delicious, this is the quintessential Irish main course.
Traditionally, mutton chops are used, but you can use lamb instead.

Serves 4

INGREDIENTS
1.25 kg/2¾ lb boneless lamb chops
15 ml/1 tbsp vegetable oil
3 large onions
4 large carrots, thickly sliced
900 ml/1½ pints/3¾ cups water
4 large potatoes, unpeeled and cut
 into chunks
1 large fresh thyme sprig
15 g/½ oz/1 tbsp butter
15 ml/1 tbsp chopped fresh parsley
salt and freshly ground black pepper

2 Quarter the onions. Add to the
casserole with the carrots and cook for
5 minutes, until the onions are browned.
Return the meat to the pan with the
water. Bring to the boil, reduce the
heat, cover and simmer for 1 hour.

3 Add the potatoes to the pan,
together with the thyme sprig and
cook for a further 1 hour.

1 Trim any fat from the lamb. Heat
the oil in a flameproof casserole and
brown the meat on both sides.
Remove from the pan.

COOK'S TIP: Mutton – meat from
an animal over one year old – is still
available from some independent
butchers. It is stronger tasting and
darker in colour than lamb.

4 Leave the stew to settle for a few
minutes. Remove the fat from the
liquid with a ladle, then pour off the
liquid into a clean saucepan. Stir in the
butter and the parsley. Season well and
pour back into the casserole. Serve.

Steak with Stout & Potatoes

This recipe uses the finest and most famous of all the Emerald Isle's ingredients: Irish beef, Murphy's stout and, of course, potatoes.

Serves 4

INGREDIENTS
675 g/1½ lb stewing or braising steak
15 ml/1 tbsp vegetable oil
25 g/1 oz/2 tbsp butter
225 g/8 oz baby or pickling onions
175 ml/6 fl oz/¾ cup stout
300 ml/½ pint/1¼ cups beef stock
bouquet garni
675 g/1½ lb potatoes, cut into thick slices
225 g/8 oz field mushrooms,
    sliced if large
15 g/½ oz/2 tbsp plain flour
2.5 ml/½ tsp mild mustard
salt and freshly ground black pepper
chopped fresh thyme sprigs,
    to garnish

2 Add the baby onions to the pan and brown for 3–4 minutes, stirring occasionally. Return the steak to the pan. Pour over the stout and beef stock and season to taste with salt and freshly ground black pepper.

3 Add the bouquet garni and top with the potato slices. Cover with a tight-fitting lid and simmer over a gentle heat for 1 hour.

1 Trim any excess fat from the steak and cut into four pieces. Season both sides of the meat. Heat the oil and half the butter in a large, heavy pan. Brown the meat on both sides, taking care not to burn the butter. Remove from the pan and set aside.

4 Add the field mushrooms. Replace the lid and continue to cook for a further 30 minutes. Remove the meat and vegetables with a slotted spoon and arrange on a platter.

5 Mix the remaining butter with the flour to make a roux. Whisk a little at a time into the cooking liquid. Stir in the mustard. Cook for 2–3 minutes, until thickened. Season and pour over the meat. Garnish with plenty of thyme sprigs.

COOK'S TIP: To peel the baby onions, put them in a bowl and cover with boiling water. Leave to soak for about 5 minutes and drain. The skins should peel away easily.

Guinness & Oyster Pie

Layers of crisp puff pastry encase a tasty rich stew of tender beef and fresh oysters. An ideal dish for cold winter evenings, served with fresh vegetables.

Serves 4

INGREDIENTS
450 g/1 lb stewing or braising steak
25 g/1 oz/¼ cup plain flour
15 ml/1 tbsp vegetable oil
25 g/1 oz/2 tbsp butter
1 onion, sliced
150 ml/¼ pint/⅔ cup Guinness
150 ml/¼ pint/⅔ cup beef stock
5 ml/1 tsp sugar
bouquet garni
12 oysters, opened
350 g/12 oz puff pastry, thawed if frozen
1 egg, beaten
salt and freshly ground
    black pepper
chopped fresh parsley,
    to garnish

2 Heat the oil and butter in a flameproof casserole and fry the meat for 10 minutes, until well sealed and browned all over. Add the onion and continue cooking for 2–3 minutes, until just softened.

3 Pour in the Guinness and beef stock. Add the sugar and bouquet garni. Cover and cook in the oven for 1¼ hours.

4 Remove from the oven, spoon into a pie dish (about 1.2 litres/2 pints/5 cups) and leave to cool for 15 minutes. Increase the oven temperature to 200°C/400°F/Gas 6.

5 Meanwhile, remove the oysters from their shells and wash. Dry on kitchen paper and stir into the steak and Guinness.

1 Preheat the oven to 180°C/350°F/Gas 4. Trim any excess fat from the meat and cut into 2.5 cm/1 in cubes. Place in a plastic bag with the flour and plenty of seasoning. Shake until the meat is well coated.

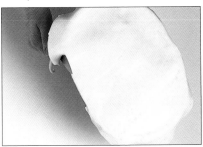

6 Roll out the pastry large enough to fit the pie dish. Brush the edge of the dish with beaten egg and lay the pastry over the top. Trim neatly and decorate. Brush with the remaining egg and cook for 25 minutes, until puffed and golden. Serve immediately, garnished with parsley.

Spiced Beef

Christmas in Ireland would not be complete without a cold side of spiced beef to see you through the holiday season.

Serves 8

INGREDIENTS
225 g/8 oz/1 cup sea salt
1.25 kg/2¾ lb silverside of beef or brisket,
   boned and untied
50 g/2 oz/½ cup brown sugar
2.5 ml/½ tsp ground allspice
2.5 ml/½ tsp ground cloves
2. 5ml/½ tsp grated nutmeg
1 bay leaf, crushed
15 ml/1 tbsp saltpetre
50 g/2 oz/1 tbsp black treacle
2 carrots, sliced
1 onion, quartered
freshly ground black pepper
pickles and bread, to serve (optional)

2 In a bowl, mix the brown sugar, ground allspice and cloves, nutmeg, bay leaf, saltpetre and pepper. Remove the beef from the salt and juices and wipe dry with kitchen paper. Sprinkle with the spice mixture and leave in a cool place overnight.

3 Lightly warm the black treacle and pour it over the spiced meat. Leave to marinate for 1 week, turning once a day.

1 Rub the salt into the beef and leave in a cool place overnight.

COOK'S TIP: Saltpetre is the common name for potassium nitrate, a powerful bactericide used for preserving raw meat.

4 Roll up the beef and secure it with string. Put it into a large pan of boiling water with the carrots and onion. Bring to the boil, lower the heat, cover and simmer for 3 hours. Leave to cool in the liquid.

5 Transfer the cooled beef to a board or a large plate. Balance another board on top, weigh it down and leave for at least 8 hours. Carve and serve the meat cold with pickles and bread, if liked.

Potato & Swede Stuffing

An unusual and delicious alternative to traditional stuffings. This amount is enough to fill a 2.75 kg/6 lb turkey.

Serves 8

INGREDIENTS
900 g/2 lb potatoes
1 large swede
115 g/4 oz/½ cup butter
4 streaky bacon rashers,
    finely chopped
1 large onion, finely chopped
1 large fresh thyme sprig
salt and freshly ground
    black pepper

1 Cut the potatoes into large equal-size pieces. Place in a saucepan and cover with cold water. Bring to the boil, reduce the heat and cover. Cook for 20 minutes.

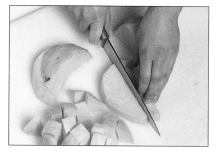

2 Meanwhile, cut the swede into chunks. Place in a saucepan and cover with cold water. Bring to the boil, reduce the heat and cook for 20 minutes.

3 Drain both the potatoes and swede and dry out over a high heat for 1 minute, until all traces of moisture have evaporated. Transfer to a bowl.

4 Melt the butter in a pan and fry the bacon for 3–4 minutes. Add the chopped onion and fry for a further 3–4 minutes, until soft. Sprinkle over the thyme leaves.

VARIATION: Two sliced carrots can be added to the swede for the last 10 minutes of cooking.

5 Stir into the vegetables. Season well and mash until smooth. Use to stuff turkey and roasts as usual, or put into an ovenproof dish and cover with foil. Bake in the oven for the final hour of the meat's cooking time.

Champ

Simple but undeniably tasty, champ makes an excellent accompaniment to a hearty stew. Use a floury potato, such as King Edward.

Serves 4

INGREDIENTS
900 g/2 lb potatoes
1 small bunch spring onions
150 ml/¼ pint/⅔ cup milk
50 g/2 oz/4 tbsp butter
salt and freshly ground
    black pepper

2 Cut the green stems from the spring onions and set aside. Finely chop the remaining onions and put them into a saucepan with the milk. Bring to the boil and simmer until just soft.

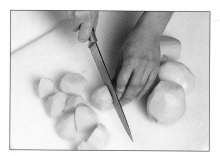

1 Cut the potatoes into even-size chunks, place in a pan and cover with cold water. Bring to the boil, reduce the heat, cover and simmer for 20 minutes, until tender.

COOK'S TIP: When buying spring onions, look for firm, white bases and undamaged green tops. They should be clean, with no sliminess, which indicates that they are no longer fresh. The mildest spring onions are the slimmest.

3 Drain the potatoes well and put them back into the saucepan. Return to the heat for 1 minute, until all traces of moisture have evaporated.

4 Mash the potatoes with the milk and onions and season well. Serve with the butter melting on top and garnish with the chopped green stems of the spring onions.

Colcannon

A famous and delicious southern Irish dish which is traditionally served with grilled sausages and bacon.

Serves 4

INGREDIENTS
900 g/2 lb potatoes
1 Savoy cabbage
50 g/2 oz/¼ cup butter
1 small onion, finely chopped
15 ml/1 tbsp chopped
   fresh parsley
salt and freshly ground
   black pepper

1 Cut the potatoes into equal-size chunks. Place in a saucepan and cover with cold water. Bring to the boil, reduce the heat, cover and simmer for 20 minutes.

VARIATION: Other varieties of green cabbage, such as pointed and drumhead cabbages, also work well in this recipe. However, do not use red or white cabbages, which have tougher leaves and require longer cooking times.

2 Drain the potatoes and dry out over a high heat for 1 minute, until all traces of moisture have evaporated, then mash them.

3 Meanwhile, bring another pan of water to the boil. Break off the outer cabbage leaves and discard. Tear the remaining leaves into pieces and cook in the boiling water for 15 minutes, until just tender.

4 Melt the butter in a large frying pan and heat until hot. Add the chopped onion and cook for 3–4 minutes, until just soft.

5 Add the mashed potato and cabbage and fry for 5 minutes, stirring occasionally until it begins to brown around the edges. Stir in the chopped parsley and season well.

Griddle Cakes

Also called potato cakes or scones, these are delicious served hot with butter and jam, or with grilled bacon for a hearty breakfast.

Makes 6

INGREDIENTS
225 g/8 oz potatoes
115 g/4 oz/1 cup plain flour
1.5 ml/¼ tsp salt
1.5 ml/¼ tsp baking powder
15 g/½ oz/1 tbsp butter, plus extra,
   for frying
25 ml/1½ tbsp milk

1 Cut the potatoes into equal-size chunks. Place in a saucepan and cover with cold water. Bring to the boil, reduce the heat, cover and simmer for 20 minutes, until tender.

2 Drain the potatoes and dry out over a high heat for 1 minute, until all traces of moisture have evaporated. Mash well, making sure there are no lumps left.

3 Sift the flour, salt and baking powder into a bowl. Rub in the butter with your fingertips until combined.

4 Add the mashed potato and mix thoroughly with a fork. Make a well in the centre and pour in the milk. Bring the mixture together to form a smooth dough.

5 Turn out on to a floured board and knead. Roll out to a round 5 mm/ ¼ in thick. Cut in half, then cut each half into three triangles.

6 Grease a griddle or large frying pan with some butter and heat until very hot. Fry the cakes for about 3–4 minutes, until golden brown, turning once during cooking, then serve hot.

Chocolate Carragheen with Irish Coffee Sauce

An impressive-looking dessert that is extremely simple to make. The secret ingredient is sure to keep dinner-party guests guessing.

Serves 4

INGREDIENTS
600 ml/1 pint/2½ cups full-cream milk
20 g/¾ oz carragheen moss
250 g/9 oz/1¼ cups sugar
115 g/4 oz plain chocolate
2.5 ml/½ tsp groundnut oil
90 ml/6 tbsp water
250 ml/8 fl oz/1 cup strong coffee
15 ml/1 tbsp Irish whiskey
grated chocolate and lightly whipped
    cream, to serve

1 Pour the milk into a heavy-based saucepan. Add the moss and 25 g/1 oz/ 2 tbsp of sugar. Bring to the boil. Reduce the heat and simmer for 15 minutes.

2 Meanwhile, using a sharp chopping knife, chop the chocolate into small pieces or grate roughly. Remove the milk from the heat and stir in the chocolate until it has all melted.

3 Strain the chocolate mixture through a fine strainer. Very lightly grease four teacups with groundnut oil, then pour in the chocolate carragheen. Chill until set.

4 Pour the water and remaining sugar into a heavy-based saucepan. Heat gently, stirring until the sugar dissolves. Remove the spoon and continue to heat the syrup until it turns a pale golden colour.

COOK'S TIP: It is best to use an Irish whiskey to make the sauce, as it has a distinctive flavour that is unlike Scotch, American or Canadian versions. Branded Irish whiskey is never blended and has to be matured for a minimum of five years.

5 Pour in the coffee and stir over a gentle heat until smooth. Remove from the heat and cool. Stir in the whiskey. Leave to cool.

6 Turn each mousse on to a plate and pour some sauce around each one. Serve decorated with the grated chocolate and cream.

Bread Pudding

This moist fruit pudding is delicious served hot or cold, cut into slices.

Serves 4–6

INGREDIENTS
450 g/1 lb stale white bread, thickly sliced
225 g/8 oz/1⅓ cups dried fruit
175 g/6 oz/¾ cup brown sugar
grated rind of 1 lemon
5 ml/1 tsp mixed spice
3 eggs, beaten
15 g/½ oz/1 tbsp butter
single cream and brown sugar, to serve

1 Grease a 20 cm/8 in round cake tin. Put the bread into a bowl and soak in plenty of water (about 1.2 litres/ 2 pints/5 cups) for 30 minutes. Drain off the water and squeeze out the excess moisture from the bread. Preheat the oven to 180°C/350°F/Gas 4.

2 Mash the bread with a fork and stir in the dried fruit, sugar, lemon rind, mixed spice and eggs, mixing well.

3 Spoon the mixture into the cake tin. Dot the top of the pudding with butter, then bake for 1½ hours. Serve warm or leave until completely cool and cut into slices. Serve with single cream and brown sugar.

Marmalade Pudding

Use a thick-cut peel marmalade for this delicious steamed pudding.

Serves 4–6

INGREDIENTS
115 g/4 oz/1 cup self-raising flour
pinch of salt
5 ml/1 tsp ground ginger
115 g/4 oz/1 cup shredded suet
115 g/4 oz/2 cups fresh white breadcrumbs
75 g/3 oz/6 tbsp dark brown sugar
175 g/6 oz/generous ½ cup marmalade,
   plus 60 ml/4 tbsp to serve
30 ml/2 tbsp milk
single cream and orange slices, to serve

1 Grease a 900 ml/1½ pint/3¾ cup pudding basin. Sift the flour, salt and ginger into a large bowl. Add the shredded suet, fresh breadcrumbs and sugar and mix thoroughly.

2 Add the marmalade and milk, mixing thoroughly to form a wet, dough-like mixture. Pour into the pudding basin. The mixture should three-quarters fill the basin. Cover with a double layer of greaseproof paper and secure with string.

3 Steam the pudding for 2½ hours in a double pan with a tight-fitting lid. Check the water after 1¼ hours.

4 Lift out the basin and remove the paper. Run a knife around the edge of the bowl, invert on to a plate and turn out. Warm the remaining marmalade in a small pan with 30 ml/2 tbsp water and serve with the pudding with cream and orange slices.

Pralie Apple Pie with Honey

This deliciously sweet apple pie is made with potato pastry which cooks to a thin crisp crust that melts in the mouth.

Serves 4

INGREDIENTS
225 g/8 oz potatoes
115 g/4 oz/1 cup plain flour
75 g/3 oz/6 tbsp caster sugar
2.5 ml/½ tsp baking powder
pinch of salt
2 cooking apples
1 egg, beaten
30 ml/2 tbsp clear honey,
    to serve

1 Cut the potatoes into even-size chunks. Put into a saucepan and bring to the boil, then cover and cook for 20 minutes.

2 Drain the potatoes and dry out over a high heat for 1 minute, until all traces of moisture have evaporated. Mash well in a bowl. Preheat the oven to 180°C/350°F/Gas 4.

3 Add the flour, 50 g/2 oz/4 tbsp of the sugar, the baking powder and salt and mix to form a soft dough.

4 Place the dough on a lightly floured surface and divide it in half. Roll out one half to a 20 cm/8 in round. Transfer to a lightly greased baking tray.

5 Peel, core and thinly slice the apples. Arrange them on top of the pastry. Sprinkle with the remaining sugar. Brush the edges of the pastry with beaten egg.

COOK'S TIP: For best results, use a variety of cooking apple, such as Sturmer Pippin or McIntosh, that retains its texture when cooked. Alternatively, use an "all-round" eating apple, such as Egremont Russet, Granny Smith or Jonathan.

6 Roll out the remaining pastry to a 25 cm/10 in round, then lay it over the apples. Seal the pastry edges together and brush with the remaining beaten egg.

7 Bake for 30 minutes, until golden. Serve hot in slices, with a little honey drizzled over each serving.

Carrot Pudding

A light steamed pudding made with grated carrot, plump sultanas and a
hint of orange. The grated carrot makes the pudding beautifully moist.

Serves 4

INGREDIENTS
50 g/2 oz/½ cup self-raising flour
5 ml/1 tsp baking powder
pinch of grated nutmeg
1 carrot
50 g/2 oz/1 cup fresh white breadcrumbs
50 g/2 oz/½ cup shredded
   vegetable suet
50 g/2 oz/4 tbsp sultanas
grated rind of 1 orange
1 egg
120 ml/4 fl oz/½ cup semi-skimmed milk
caster sugar and whipped cream,
   to serve

1 Lightly grease a 900 ml/1½ pint/
3¾ cup pudding basin. Sift the flour,
baking powder and nutmeg into a
mixing bowl.

2 Finely grate the carrot and add to
the flour mixture. Stir in the fresh
breadcrumbs, shredded suet, sultanas
and orange rind.

3 Beat the egg and the milk together,
then stir into the dry ingredients to
form a smooth dropping consistency.

4 Spoon the mixture into the prepared
pudding basin. Cover the basin with
two layers of greaseproof paper, folded
in the middle to allow room for
expansion, and secure with string.

5 Steam for 2 hours in a double pan
with a tight-fitting lid. Check the
water after 1 hour and top up, if
necessary. Remove the greaseproof
paper and turn out the pudding on to
a plate. Dust with a little caster sugar
and serve with whipped cream.

Soda Bread

Fresh home-made soda bread makes the perfect accompaniment to hearty dishes, such as Leek & Thyme Soup and Coddle.

Makes 1 loaf

INGREDIENTS
450 g/1 lb/4 cups plain flour
5 ml/1 tsp salt
5 ml/1 tsp bicarbonate of soda
400 ml/14 fl oz/1⅔ cups buttermilk

1 Preheat the oven to 230°C/450°F/ Gas 8. Sift the plain flour, salt and bicarbonate of soda into a large bowl. Make a well in the centre and pour in the buttermilk.

3 Turn on to a floured board and knead lightly for 1 minute, until smooth. Smooth and shape to a round about 4 cm/1½ in high. Cut a deep cross from one edge to the other. Place on a floured baking tray.

2 Using one hand, slowly incorporate the flour into the milk to give a soft, but not sticky, dough.

4 Bake for 15 minutes. Reduce the heat to 200°C/400°F/Gas 6 and bake for a further 30 minutes. To test if the bread is cooked, tap the underside of the loaf, which should sound hollow. Cool on a wire rack.

VARIATION: For good soda bread it's important to use buttermilk as its reaction with the bicarbonate of soda helps the bread rise. If you can't buy buttermilk, use sour milk or sour your own fresh milk with a few teaspoons of lemon juice.

Barm Brack

This traditional Hallowe'en cake would once have had a ring baked inside.

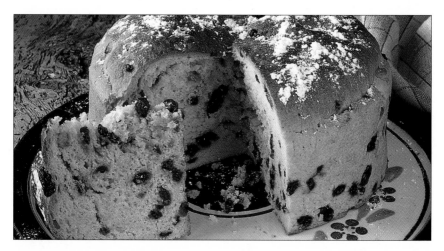

Makes a 23 cm/9 in cake

INGREDIENTS
675 g/1½ lb/6 cups plain flour
2.5 ml/½ tsp mixed spice
5 ml/1 tsp salt
10 g/¼ oz easy-blend dried yeast
50 g/2 oz/¼ cup caster sugar
300 ml/½ pint/1¼ cups warm milk
150 ml/¼ pint/⅔ cup warm water
50 g/2 oz/4 tbsp butter, softened
50 g/2 oz/4 tbsp currants
225 g/8 oz/1½ cups sultanas
50 g/2 oz/5 tbsp chopped peel
milk or syrup, to glaze
icing sugar, to decorate

1 Grease a 23 cm/9 in round cake tin. Sift the flour, mixed spice and salt together. Stir in the yeast and 15 ml/ 1 tbsp of the sugar.

2 Make a well, then pour in the milk and water and mix to a dough. Transfer to a floured board and knead until smooth and no longer sticky. Place in a clean bowl, cover with clear film and leave in a warm place for 1 hour, until well risen and doubled in size.

3 Add the butter, currants, sultanas and chopped peel and work into the dough. Return to the bowl and cover. Leave for another 30 minutes. Preheat the oven to 200°C/400°F/Gas 6.

4 Fit the dough into the tin and leave to rise to the top. Brush with milk or syrup and bake for 15 minutes. Cover with foil. Reduce the heat to 180°C/ 350°F/Gas 4 and bake for 45 minutes. Dust with icing sugar.

Irish Coffee

This classic Irish beverage is included in the dessert section because, as the Irish say, "there's eating and drinking in it!"

Makes 4

INGREDIENTS
20 ml/4 tsp granulated sugar
600 ml/1 pint/2½ cups strong hot coffee
4 measures Irish whiskey
300 ml/½ pint/1¼ cups thick double cream

1 Divide the granulated sugar among four stemmed, heatproof glasses. Put a metal teaspoon in each glass.

2 Carefully pour in the hot coffee and stir to dissolve the sugar.

3 Stir a measure of whiskey into each glass. Remove the teaspoon and hold it upside-down over the glass.

4 Slowly pour the double cream over the back of the spoon on to the hot coffee so that it floats on the surface. Serve at once.

This edition is published by Southwater

Distributed in the UK by
The Manning Partnership,
251–253 London Road East, Batheaston,
Bath BA1 7RL, UK
tel. (0044) 01225 852 727
fax (0044) 01225 852 852

Distributed in Australia by
Sandstone Publishing,
Unit 1, 360 Norton Street, Leichhardt,
New South Wales 2040, Australia
tel. (0061) 2 9560 7888
fax (0061) 2 9560 7488

Distributed in New Zealand by
Five Mile Press NZ,
PO Box 33–1071, Takapuna,
Auckland 9, New Zealand
tel. (0064) 9 4444 144
fax (0064) 9 4444 518

Southwater is an imprint of Anness Publishing Limited

© 2000 Anness Publishing Limited

Publisher: Joanna Lorenz

Editor: Valerie Ferguson

Series Designer: Bobbie Colgate Stone

Designer: Andrew Heath

Editorial Reader: Marion Wilson

Production Controller: Joanna King

Recipes contributed by: Matthew Drennan

Photography: Thomas Odulate

1 3 5 7 9 10 8 6 4 2

Notes:
For all recipes, quantities are given in both metric
and imperial measures and, where appropriate,
measures are also given in standard cups
and spoons.
Follow one set, but not a mixture, because they
are not interchangeable.

Standard spoon and cup measures are level.

1 tsp = 5 ml   1 tbsp = 15 ml

1 cup = 250 ml/8 fl oz

Australian standard tablespoons are 20 ml.
Australian readers should use 3 tsp in place of
1 tbsp for measuring small quantities of gelatine,
cornflour, salt, etc.

Medium eggs are used unless otherwise stated.

64